THE UNOFFICIAL CHRISTMAS TRUCE OF 1914

History of the World

Children's Military Books

Speedy Publishing LLC

40 E. Main St. #1156

Newark, DE 19711

www.speedypublishing.com

Copyright 2017

In this book, we're going to talk about the unofficial Christmas truce of 1914. So, let's get right to it!

World War I began in July of 1914. At the beginning, many people believed that the battle would be quick and that soldiers would be home before Christmas. However, by the time November had come, it was evident that the war was not going to end soon. Britain's soldiers were absolutely exhausted after the many months of life in the trenches.

World War 1

Trench Warfare

LIVE AND LET LIVE

Trench warfare was slow and between times when active fighting was going on, the soldiers were very bored. The enemy's trenches were sometimes only a few yards away. Every day, in addition to the fighting, there were practical matters to attend to. In between the trench lines was an area called "No Man's Land."

If a soldier was shot and wounded outside the trenches, he would have to be brought back to the trenches. If he had died out there, his body would also need to be retrieved and buried.

Soldiers in Trench

In addition to these difficult tasks, the soldiers also needed time to eat regular meals from the food wagons and to gather supplies, such as food, water, and ammunition. Sometimes a period of time was set aside to make construction repairs within the trenches.

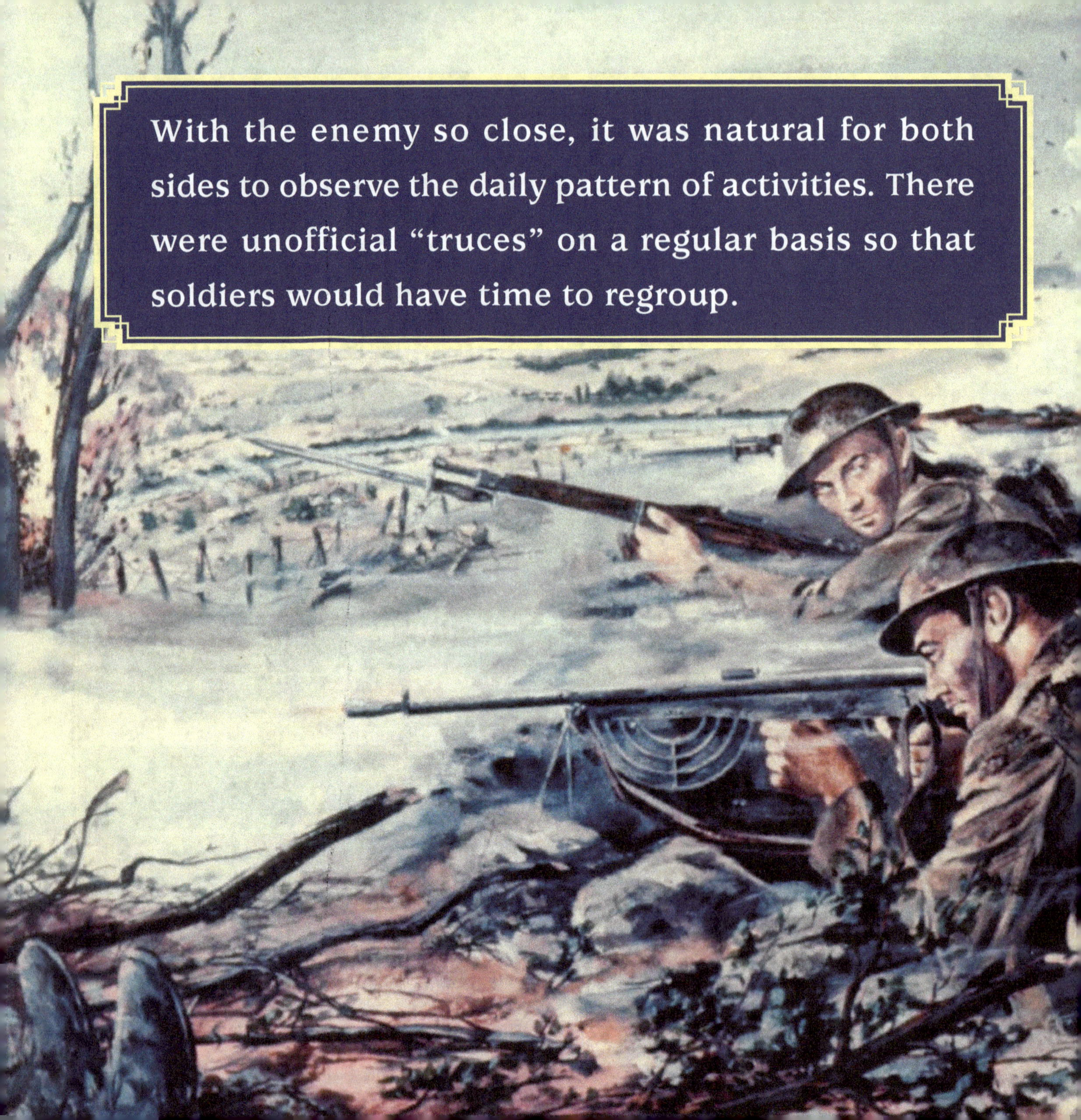

With the enemy so close, it was natural for both sides to observe the daily pattern of activities. There were unofficial "truces" on a regular basis so that soldiers would have time to regroup.

World War 1

World War 1

Sometimes during these "quiet periods," soldiers would emerge from the unsanitary, stifling trenches to get a breath of fresh air. Enemies would talk with each other and sometimes even barter for packs of cigarettes across enemy lines. A "live and let live" attitude happened in different areas at different times.

The leaders on both sides were concerned about these "friendly" activities. After all, it's difficult to maintain a battle mindset if you feel as if you and your enemy have a lot in common. Engaging in conversation or exchanges with the enemy, called "fraternizing with the enemy" were considered to be acts of treason. However, the top leaders weren't always around to supervise and the battles couldn't go on 24 hours a day, 7 days a week, so there were times when signals were given and the fighting stopped for a while.

World War 1 Christmas Truce

Monument of Pope Benedict XV

POPE BENEDICT XV
SUGGESTS A TRUCE

When Benedict XV became pope in September, he made a plea for a Christmas truce, but his suggestion was rejected by both sides. The soldiers were tired of the fighting and missed their families. Daily life within the wet, cold, smelly trenches was so depressing. They longed for the warmth of their fireplaces and the sights and sounds of Christmas. All along the Western front, small miracles began to happen.

No one knows who started it or exactly how it started. In many cases, it seemed to happen almost spontaneously. The families back at home found out what had occurred when soldiers wrote to tell them what had happened.

Christmas Truce 1914

Christmas Truce 1914

Historians who have reviewed oral testimony, journal entries, and handwritten letters from the soldiers have pieced together what occurred, but the story is a patchwork of different events as each local region celebrated differently. Not all areas observed the "unofficial truce." Many areas continued to fire shots and proceeded with heavy fighting.

At this point in the war it was primarily British, Belgian, and French soldiers fighting for the Allied Powers against their enemies, the Germans who were part of the Central Powers. Less of these truces sprung up between the French, Belgian, and German soldiers since the Germans had invaded their countries.

World War 1

British WW1 Soldiers

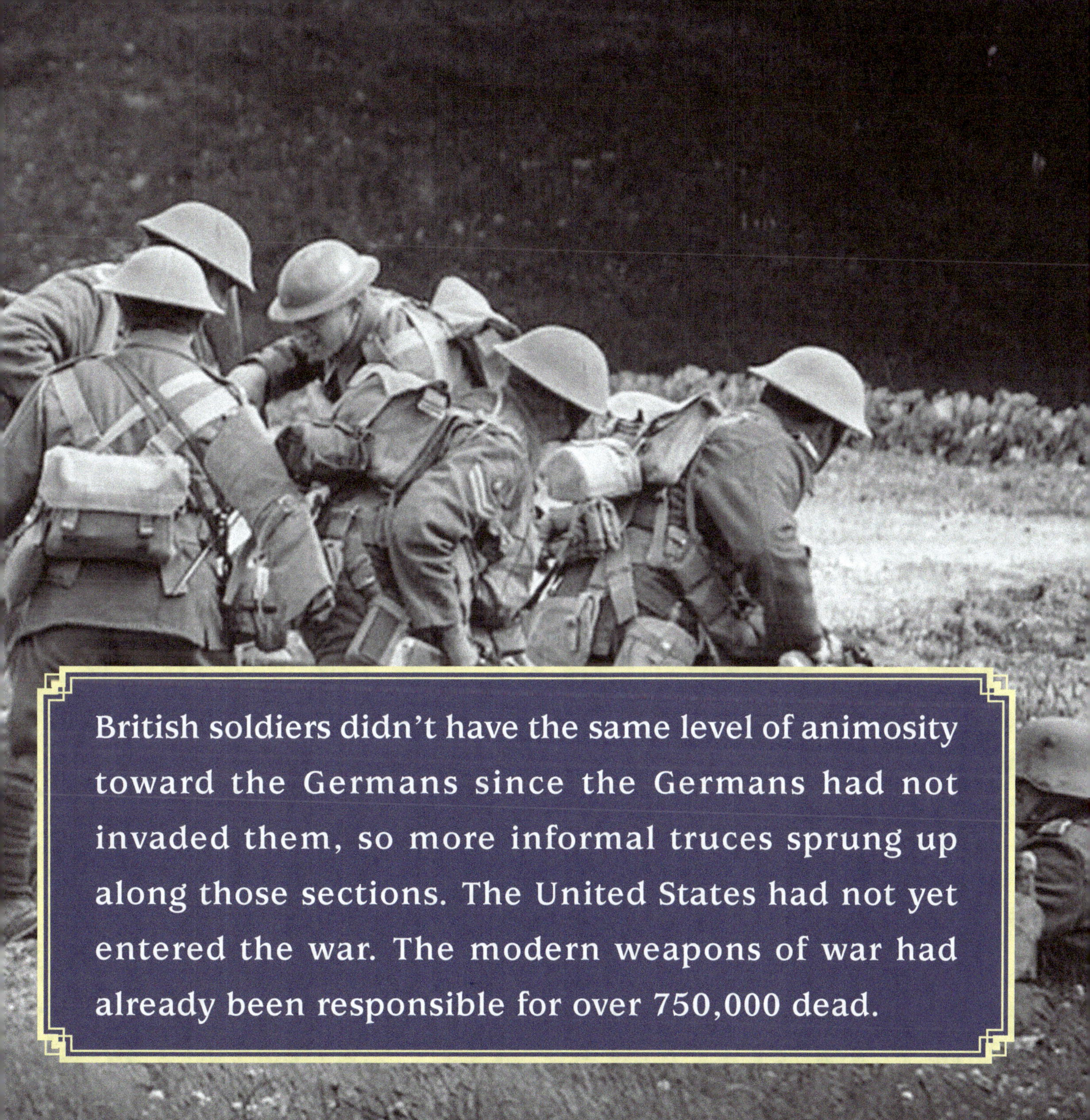

British soldiers didn't have the same level of animosity toward the Germans since the Germans had not invaded them, so more informal truces sprung up along those sections. The United States had not yet entered the war. The modern weapons of war had already been responsible for over 750,000 dead.

In the month of December, German leaders shipped thousands of small Christmas trees to the German troops. Their goal was to keep the morale of the German soldiers up, but it did the opposite, since the celebration of Christmas was something the enemies had in common with each other.

Christmas Truce Memorial Ceremony

Christmas Truce 1914 Memorial

Many accounts of the event state that it began on Christmas Eve. It was a bright, moonlit night. There was a layer of white frost on the ground. Then, suddenly from the German side, there were sounds of a Christmas carol being sung. After the German singing stopped, the British began singing a carol, and it went back and forth for a while.

At one point, the British began to sing "O Come All Ye Faithful" and the Germans replied with the Latin version of the same song "Adeste Fideles." No one could believe what was happening. As the British soldiers looked out over the trenches they could see that the Germans had put some Christmas trees up above their trench lines. Some of the trees had been placed in the feared area of "No Man's Land."

No Man's Land

GOD BLESS

CHRISTMAS DAY 1914

On Christmas Day in some locations, the Germans called out "Merry Christmas!"

The Allied soldiers slowly came out of the trenches, fearing that they might be shot. In other locations, the Germans displayed placards that said "if you no shoot, we no shoot."

No Man's Land

From dawn until dusk on Christmas Day, the soldiers spoke to each other and gave each other gifts of hats, food, and cigarettes. This informal truce also gave them time to collect their fellow soldiers whose dead bodies had been decaying in the "No Man's Land" area for weeks.

The miraculous events along the trench lines were different experiences for every group of men. Legend has it that one British soldier met up with his German barber from before the war and his barber gave him a badly needed haircut. Another story tells of a pig-roast the men shared together in the area between the trenches. Although there weren't any organized matches, some soldiers found some makeshift balls and they played impromptu games of soccer on the battlefield.

British soccer team with gas masks

World War 1

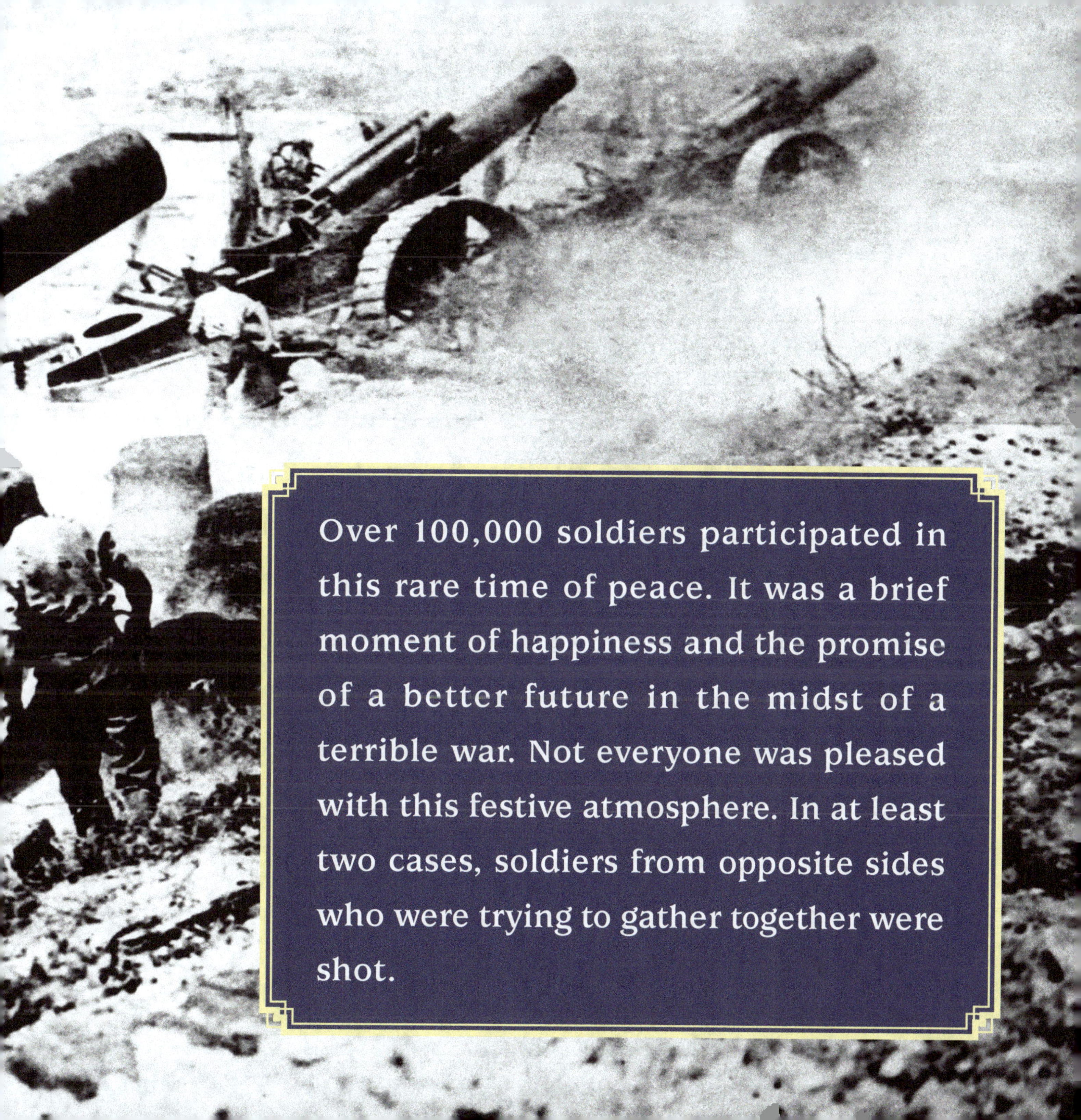

Over 100,000 soldiers participated in this rare time of peace. It was a brief moment of happiness and the promise of a better future in the midst of a terrible war. Not everyone was pleased with this festive atmosphere. In at least two cases, soldiers from opposite sides who were trying to gather together were shot.

THE FIGHTING CONTINUES

In some places, the fighting continued the day after Christmas. In a few places, the truce continued until New Year's Day. After the deafening sounds of continuous mortar shells, the silence of the truce seemed eerie. When the war resumed, it came back with full force and seemed even more brutal than it had been before. For the rest of the war, there were a few periods of peace, but never at the scale that was seen on that Christmas Eve and Christmas Day in 1914.

World War 1 weapons captured

Christmas Truce

WAS IT A MIRACLE OR WAS IT TREASON?

The leaders of the war had a different perception of these unofficial truces. The 100,000 men who had participated had defied the commands of their superiors. In some cases, "No Man's Land" was a very short distance, a 100-foot span from trench to trench.

The enemies could hear each other talking, see each other shaving, and smell each other's meals cooking. General Sir Horace Smith-Dorrien was concerned that the British Second Corps would lose their desire to fight the Germans. He sent a stern memo to the commanders of his divisions in early December warning them to punish any soldiers who were "fraternizing with the enemy."

Horace Smith-Dorrien grave

Christmas Truce site

He knew that when people live in close proximity to each other that a "live and let live" attitude can take over. It's true that many soldiers came away from the experience feeling that if the soldiers had been left to their own devices, they wouldn't have fired another shot.

Not everyone agreed with that sentiment. A young German soldier by the name of Adolf Hitler was celebrating Christmas Day in a cellar in Belgium. When he was told about the Christmas truce by men in his regiment, he screamed in outrage saying that such a thing should never happen in wartime and that the German soldiers who participated had no honor. Histories written during Hitler's World War II Nazi regime conveniently leave out any mention of the Christmas truce.

World War II

Christmas Truce

However temporary the cease in fighting was, many people around the world were inspired by the events that happened on that Christmas Eve and Christmas Day.

Christmas Truce memorial

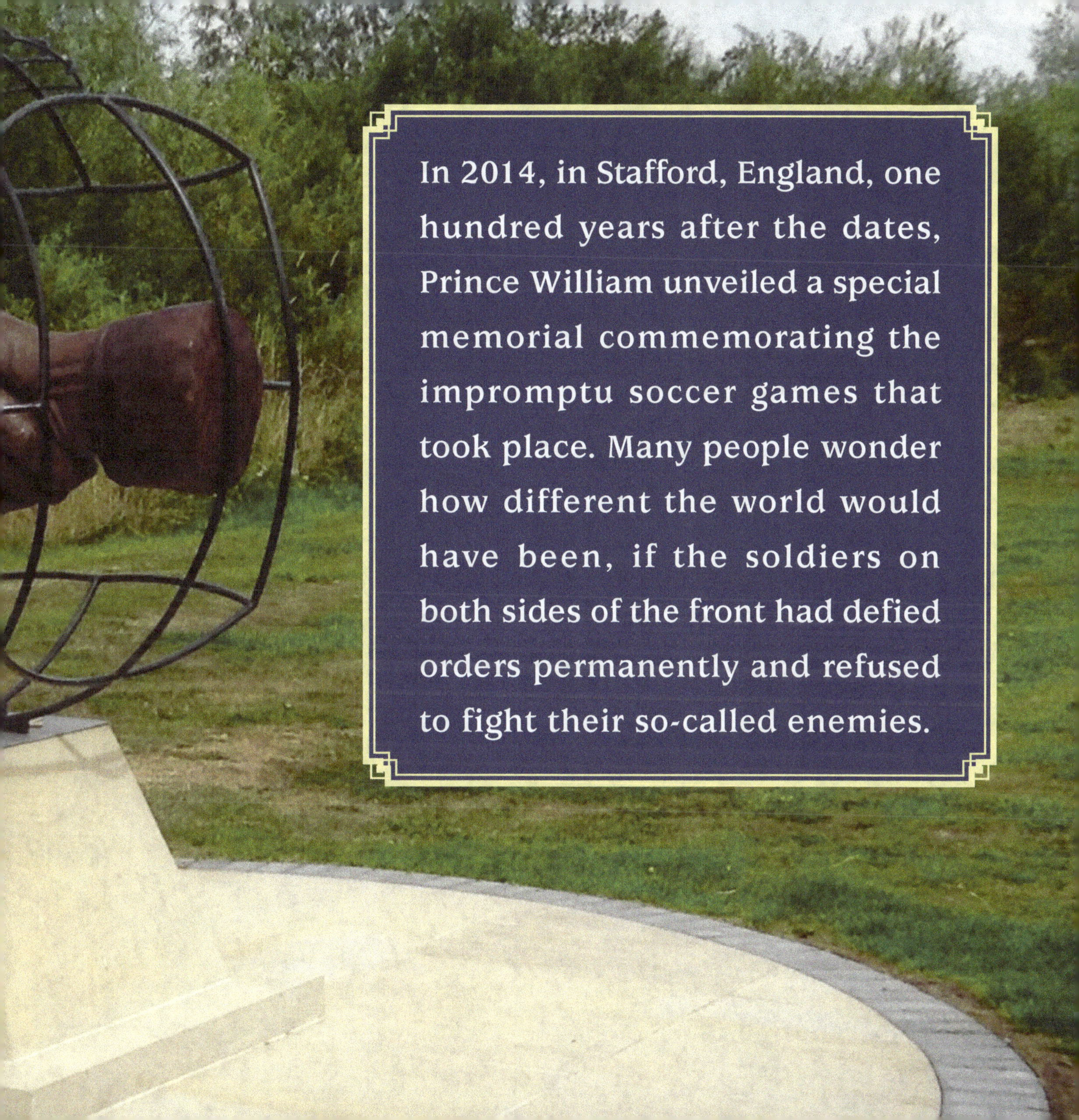

In 2014, in Stafford, England, one hundred years after the dates, Prince William unveiled a special memorial commemorating the impromptu soccer games that took place. Many people wonder how different the world would have been, if the soldiers on both sides of the front had defied orders permanently and refused to fight their so-called enemies.

Yale World War 1 Memorial

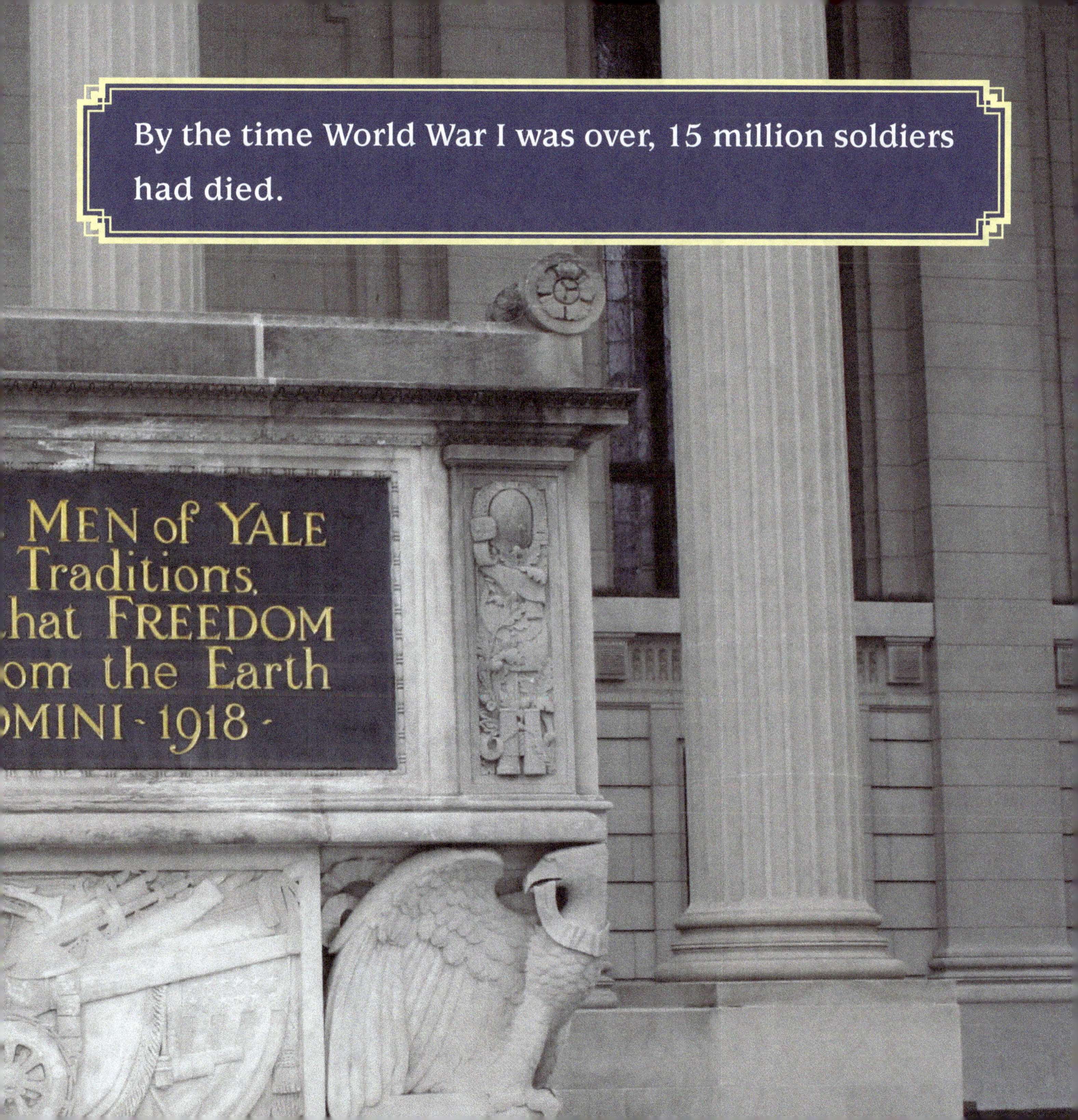

By the time World War I was over, 15 million soldiers had died.

Now you know more about the unofficial Christmas truce of 1914. You can find more Military books from Baby Professor by searching the website of your favorite book retailer.

World War I Memorial

Visit
BABY PROFESSOR
EDUCATION KIDS
www.BabyProfessorBooks.com
to download Free Baby Professor eBooks
and view our catalog of new and exciting
Children's Books